school - school	2
travel - travel	5
transport - transport	8
city - city	10
landscape - landscape	14
restaurant - restaurant	17
supermarket - supermarket	20
drinks - drinks	22
food - food	23
farm - farm	27
house - house	31
living room - living room	33
kitchen - kitchen	35
bathroom - bathroom	38
child's room - child's room	42
clothing - clothing	44
office - office	49
economy - economy	51
occupations - occupations	53
tools - tools	56
musical instruments - musical instruments	57
zoo - zoo	59
sports - sports	62
activities - activities	63
family - family	67
body - body	68
hospital - hospital	72
emergency - emergency	76
Earth - Earth	77
clock - clock	79
week - week	80
year - year	81
shapes - shapes	83
colours - colours	84
opposites - opposites	85
numbers - numbers	88
languages - languages	90
who / what / how - who / what / how	91
where - where	92

AF234913

Impressum
Verlag: BABADADA GmbH, Nedderfeld 112 , 22529 Hamburg
Geschäftsführer / Verlagsleitung: Harald Hof
Druck: Books on Demand GmbH, In de Tarpen 42, 22848 Norderstedt

Imprint
Publisher: BABADADA GmbH, Nedderfeld 112 , 22529 Hamburg, Germany
Managing Director / Publishing direction: Harald Hof
Print: Books on Demand GmbH, In de Tarpen 42, 22848 Norderstedt

school

school

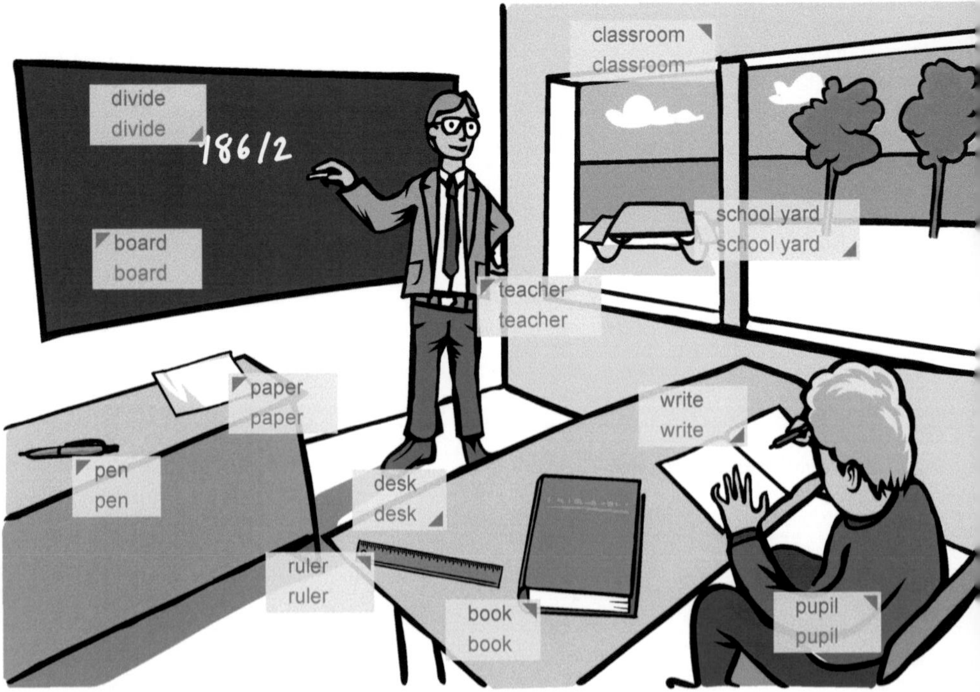
classroom
classroom
divide
divide
186/2
school yard
school yard
board
board
teacher
teacher
paper
paper
write
write
pen
pen
desk
desk
ruler
ruler
book
book
pupil
pupil

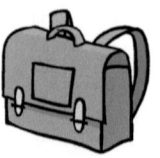

satchel
satchel

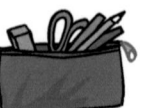

pencil case
pencil case

pencil
pencil

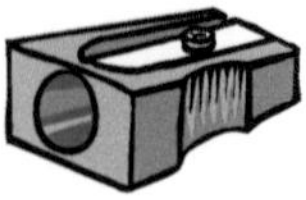

pencil sharpener
pencil sharpener

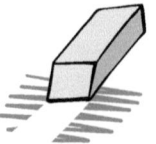

rubber
rubber

drawing pad
drawing pad

drawing

drawing

paintbrush

paintbrush

paint box

paint box

scissors

scissors

glue

glue

exercise book

exercise book

homework

homework

number

number

add

add

subtract

subtract

multiply

multiply

calculate

calculate

letter

letter

alphabet

alphabet

word

word

text
text

read
read

chalk
chalk

lesson
lesson

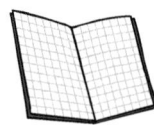

register
register

exam
exam

certificate
certificate

school uniform
school uniform

education
education

encyclopedia
encyclopedia

university
university

microscope
microscope

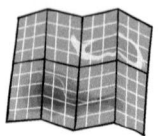

map
map

paper bin
waste-paper basket

hotel
hotel

Grand

hostel
hostel

ROOMS

bureau de change
bureau de change

ECHANGE

suitcase
suitcase

car
car

language
language

yes / no
yes / no

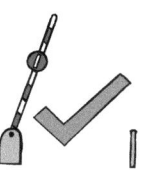

Okay
Okay

hello
hello

translator
translator

Thank you
Thank you

how much does ... cost?

how much is...?

I do not understand

I do not understand

problem

problem

Good evening!

Good evening!

Good morning!

Good morning!

Good night!

Good night!

bye bye

bye bye

direction

direction

luggage

luggage

bag

bag

backpack

backpack

guest

guest

room

room

sleeping bag

sleeping bag

tent

tent

tourist information
tourist information

beach
beach

credit card
credit card

breakfast
breakfast

lunch
lunch

dinner
dinner

ticket
ticket

lift
lift

stamp
stamp

border
border

customs
customs

embassy
embassy

visa
visa

passport
passport

transport

transport

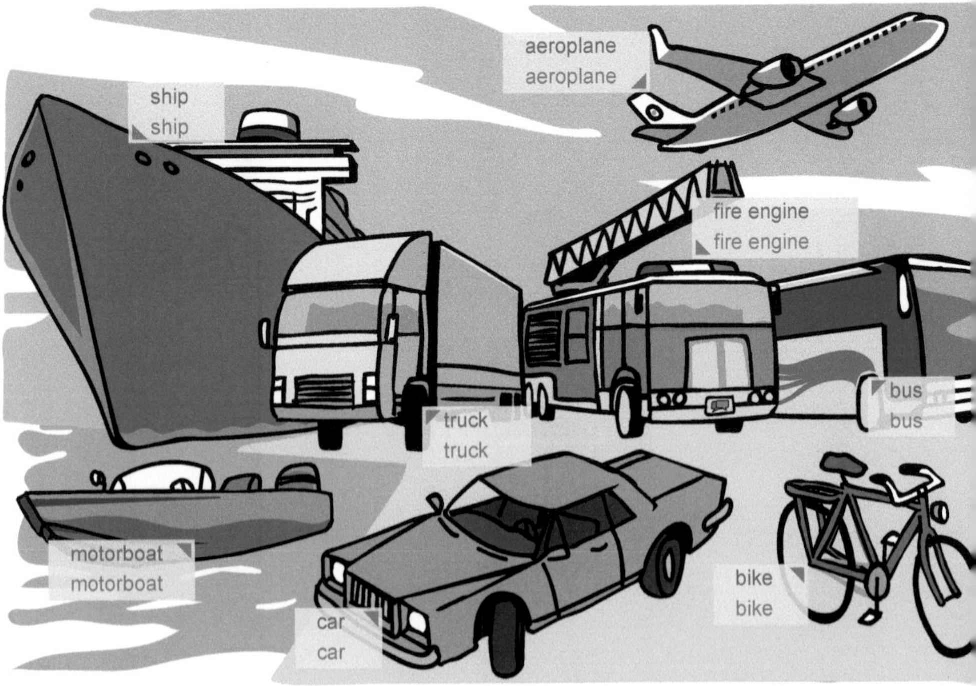
aeroplane
aeroplane
ship
ship
fire engine
fire engine
bus
bus
truck
truck
motorboat
motorboat
bike
bike
car
car

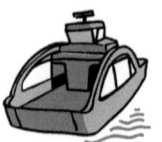

ferry

ferry

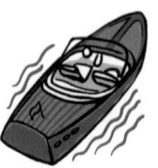

boat

boat

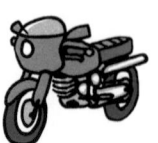

motorbike

motorbike

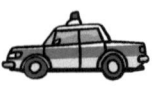

police car

police car

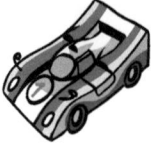

racing car

racing car

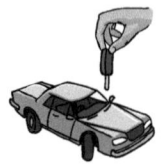

rental car

rental car

car sharing
car sharing

breakdown truck
breakdown truck

refuse truck
refuse truck

motor
motor

fuel
fuel

petrol station
petrol station

traffic sign
traffic sign

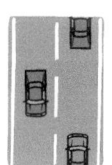

traffic
traffic

traffic jam
traffic jam

car park
car park

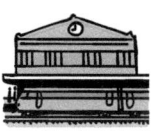

train station
train station

tracks
tracks

train
train

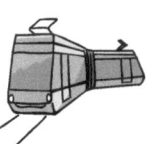

tram
tram

carriage
carriage

helicopter

helicopter

airport

airport

tower

tower

passenger

passenger

container

container

carton

carton

cart

cart

basket

basket

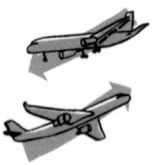

take off / land

take off / land

city

city

village

village

city centre

city centre

house

house

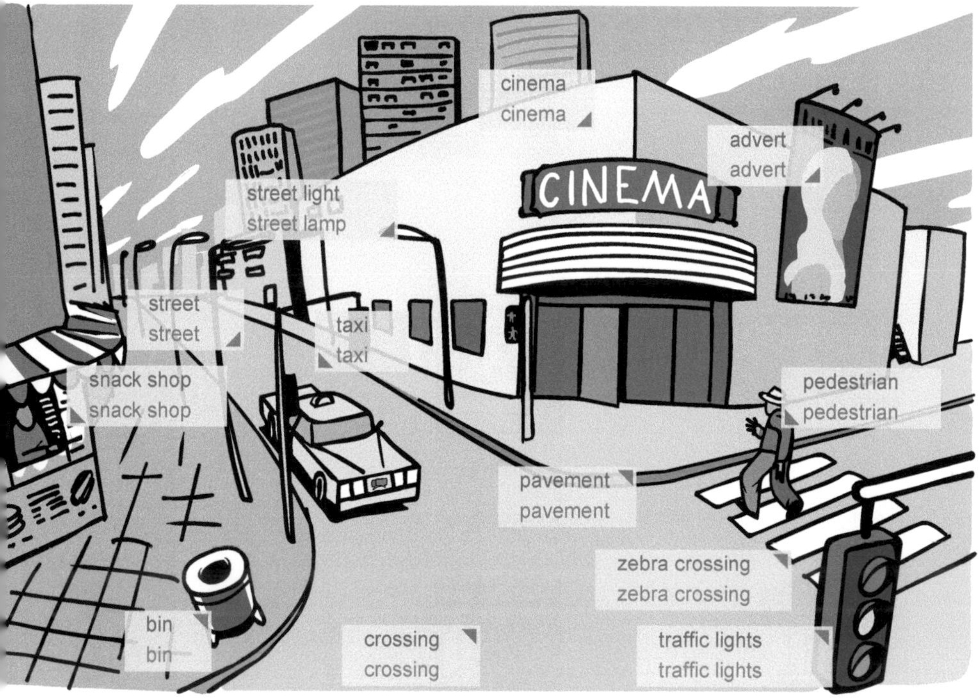

cinema
cinema
advert
advert
CINEMA
street light
street lamp
street
street
taxi
taxi
snack shop
snack shop
pedestrian
pedestrian
pavement
pavement
zebra crossing
zebra crossing
bin
bin
crossing
crossing
traffic lights
traffic lights

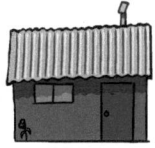

hut

hut

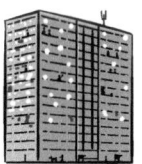

flat

flat

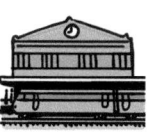

train station

train station

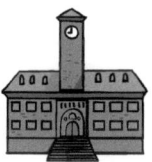

town hall

town hall

MUSEUM

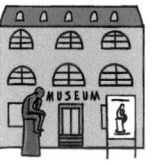

museum

museum

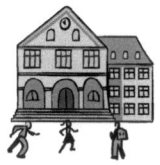

school

school

university

university

bank

bank

hospital

hospital

hotel

hotel

pharmacy

pharmacy

office

office

book shop

book shop

shop

shop

florist's

florist's

supermarket

supermarket

market

market

department store

department store

fishmonger's

fishmonger's

shopping centre

shopping centre

harbour

harbour

city - city

park
park

bench
bench

bridge
bridge

stairs
stairs

underground
underground

tunnel
tunnel

bus stop
bus stop

bar
bar

restaurant
restaurant

postbox
postbox

road sign
street sign

parking meter
parking meter

zoo
zoo

swimming pool
swimming pool

mosque
mosque

farm

farm

pollution

pollution

graveyard

graveyard

church

church

playground

playground

temple

temple

landscape

landscape

leaf
leaf

signpost
signpost

way
way

meadow
meadow

stone
stone

tree
tree

hiker
hiker

river
river

grass
grass

flower
flower

valley

valley

hill

hill

lake

lake

forest

forest

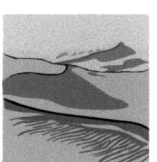

desert

desert

volcano

volcano

castle

castle

rainbow

rainbow

mushroom

mushroom

palm tree

palm tree

mosquito

mosquito

fly

fly

ant

ant

bee

bee

spider

spider

beetle
beetle

frog
frog

squirrel
squirrel

hedgehog
hedgehog

hare
hare

owl
owl

bird
bird

swan
swan

boar
boar

deer
deer

moose
moose

dam
dam

wind turbine
wind turbine

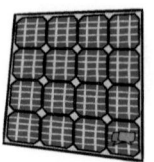

solar panel
solar panel

climate
climate

restaurant

restaurant

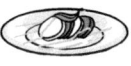

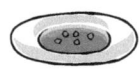

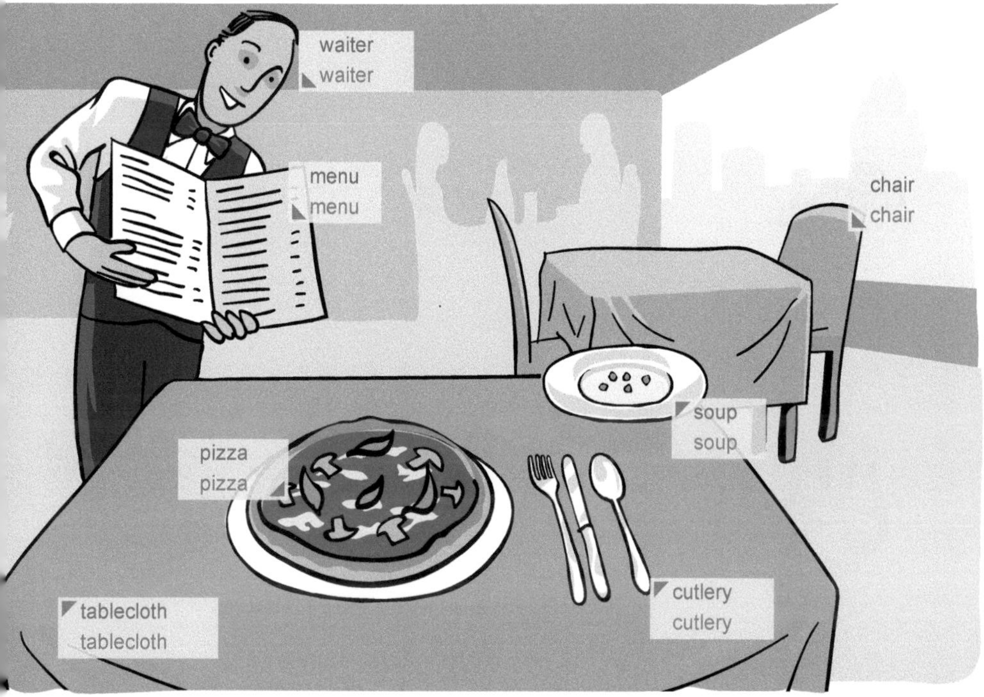

waiter
waiter
menu
menu
chair
chair
soup
soup
pizza
pizza
tablecloth
tablecloth
cutlery
cutlery

starter

starter

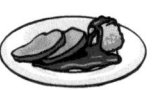

main course

main course

dessert

dessert

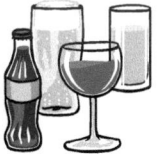

drinks

drinks

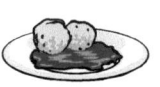

food

food

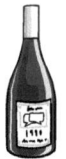

bottle

bottle

fast food

fast food

street food

street food

teapot

teapot

sugar bowl

sugar bowl

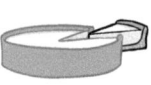

portion

portion

espresso machine

espresso machine

high chair

high chair

bill

bill

tray

tray

knife

knife

fork

fork

spoon

spoon

teaspoon

teaspoon

serviette

serviette

glass

glass

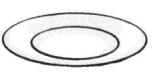

plate

plate

soup plate

soup plate

saucer

saucer

sauce

sauce

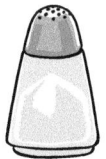

salt cellar

salt pot

pepper mill

pepper mill

vinegar

vinegar

oil

oil

spices

spices

ketchup

ketchup

mustard

mustard

mayonnaise

mayonnaise

supermarket

supermarket

special offer
special offer
FOR
customer
customer
dairy
dairy
fruit
fruit
trolley
trolley

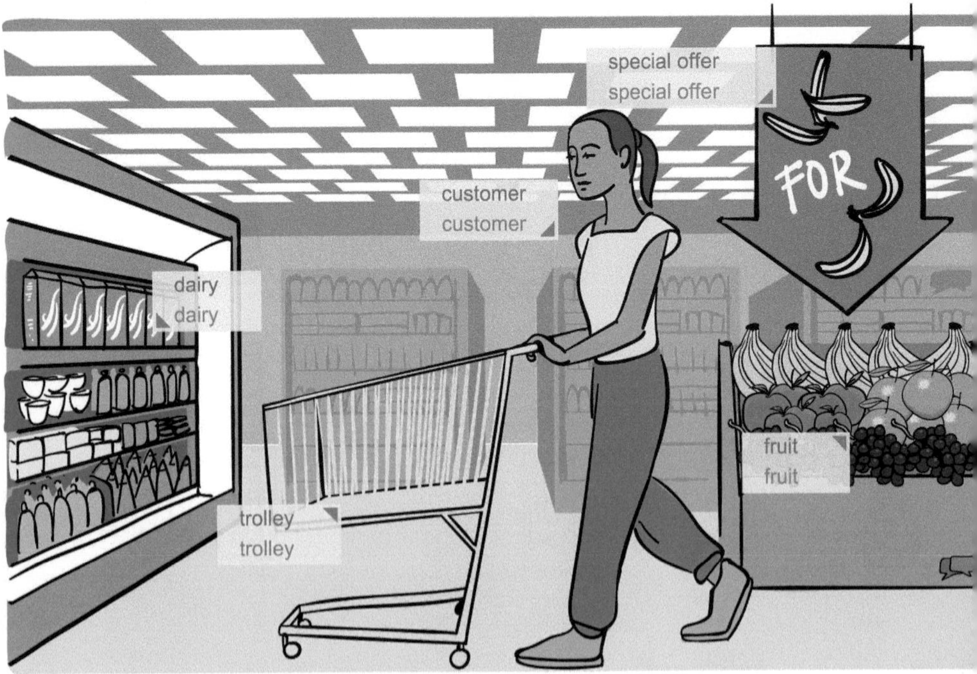

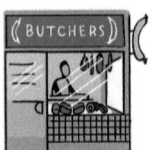

BUTCHERS

butcher´s

butcher´s

BAKERY

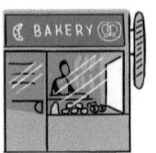

baker´s

baker´s

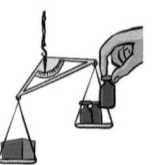

weigh

weigh

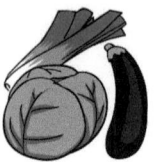

vegetables

vegetables

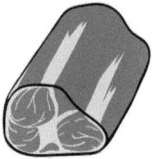

meat

meat

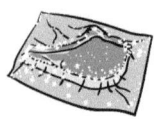

frozen food

frozen food

cold meat
cold meat

tinned food
tinned food

washing powder
washing powder

sweets
sweets

household products
household products

cleaning products
cleaning products

salesperson
salesperson

till
till

cashier
cashier

shopping list
shopping list

opening hours
opening hours

wallet
wallet

credit card
credit card

bag
bag

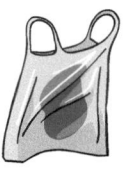

plastic bag
plastic bag

drinks

water
water

juice
juice

milk
milk

coke
coke

wine
wine

beer
beer

alcohol
alcohol

cocoa
cocoa

tea
tea

coffee
coffee

espresso
espresso

cappuccino
cappuccino

banana

banana

apple

apple

orange

orange

melon

melon

lemon

lemon

carrot

carrot

garlic

garlic

bamboo

bamboo

onion

onion

mushroom

mushroom

nuts

nuts

noodles

noodles

spaghetti

spaghetti

rice

rice

salad

salad

chips

chips

fried potatoes

fried potatoes

pizza

pizza

hamburger

hamburger

sandwich

sandwich

cutlet

cutlet

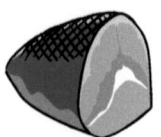

ham

ham

salami

salami

sausage

sausage

chicken

chicken

roast

roast

fish

fish

porridge oats

porridge oats

muesli

muesli

cornflakes

cornflakes

flour

flour

croissant

croissant

bread roll

bread roll

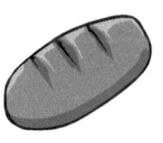

bread

bread

toast

toast

biscuits

biscuits

butter

butter

curd

curd

cake

cake

egg

egg

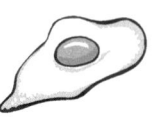

fried egg

fried egg

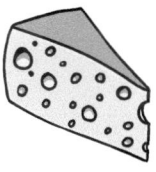

cheese

cheese

ice cream
ice cream

sugar
sugar

honey
honey

jam
jam

chocolate spread
chocolate spread

curry
curry

farmhouse
farmhouse

straw bale
straw bale

barn
barn

field
field

horse
horse

trailer
trailer

foal
foal

tractor
tractor

donkey
donkey

sheep
sheep

lamb
lamb

goat
goat

cow
cow

calf
calf

pig
pig

piglet
piglet

bull
bull

goose

goose

duck

duck

chick

chick

hen

hen

cock

cock

rat

rat

cat

cat

mouse

mouse

ox

ox

dog

dog

doghouse

doghouse

garden hose

garden hose

watering can

watering can

scythe

scythe

plough

plough

sickle

sickle

hoe

hoe

pitchfork

pitchfork

axe

axe

wheelbarrow

wheelbarrow

trough

trough

milk can

milk can

sack

sack

fence

fence

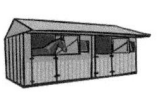

stable

stable

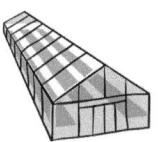

greenhouse

greenhouse

soil

soil

seed

seed

fertilizer

fertilizer

combine harvester

combine harvester

harvest

harvest

harvest

harvest

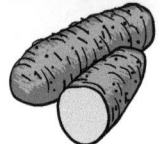

yams

yams

wheat

wheat

soy

soy

potato

potato

corn

corn

rapeseed

rapeseed

fruit tree

fruit tree

cassava

cassava

cereals

cereals

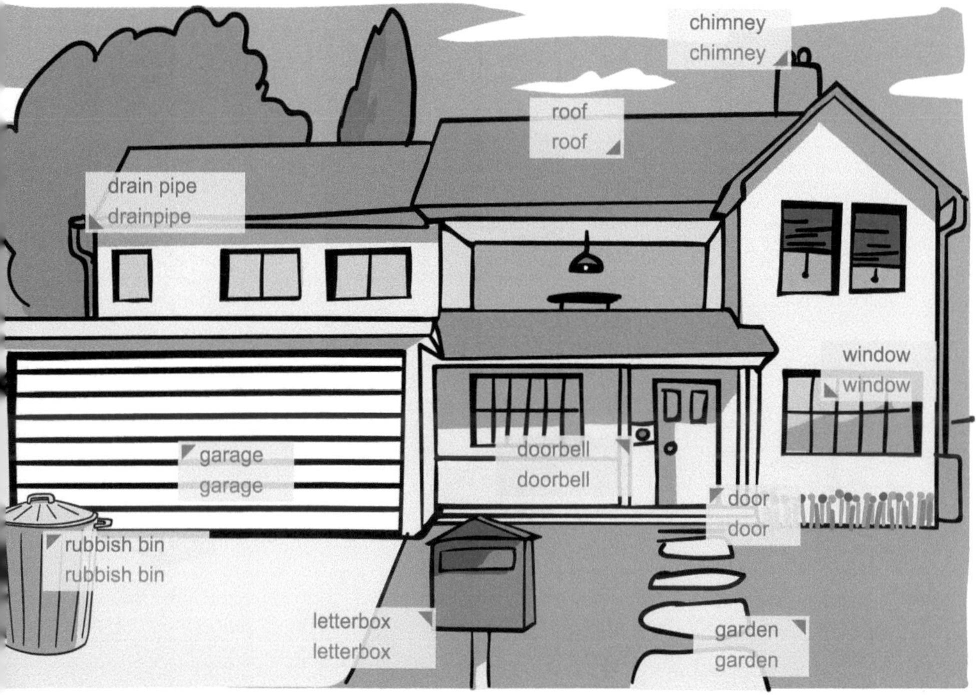

chimney
chimney

roof
roof

drain pipe
drainpipe

window
window

garage
garage

doorbell
doorbell

door
door

rubbish bin
rubbish bin

letterbox
letterbox

garden
garden

living room
living room

bathroom
bathroom

kitchen
kitchen

bedroom
bedroom

child's room
child's room

dining room
dining room

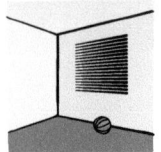

floor

floor

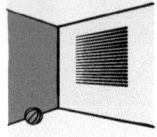

wall

wall

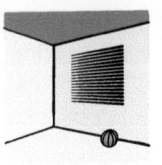

ceiling

ceiling

cellar

cellar

sauna

sauna

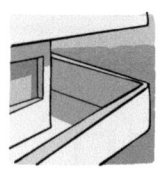

balcony

balcony

terrace

terrace

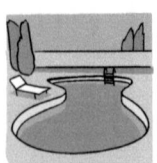

pool

pool

lawn mower

lawn mower

sheet

sheet

bedspread

bedspread

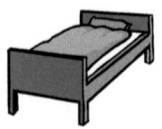

bed

bed

broom

broom

bucket

bucket

switch

switch

living room

living room

wallpaper
wallpaper
picture
picture
lamp
lamp
shelf
shelf
cupboard
cupboard
television
television
fireplace
fireplace
flower
flower
cushion
cushion
sofa
sofa
vase
vase
remote control
remote control

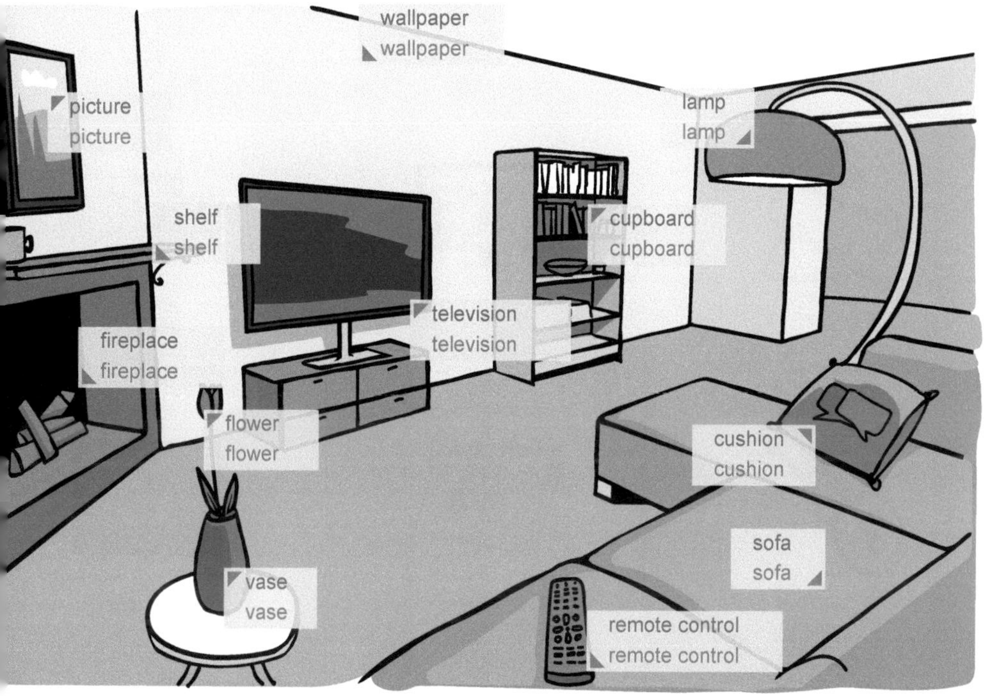

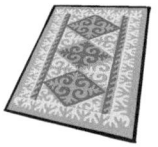

carpet

carpet

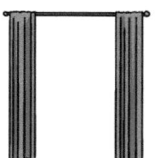

curtain

curtain

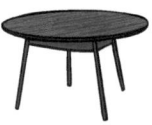

table

table

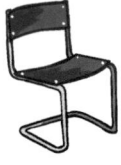

chair

chair

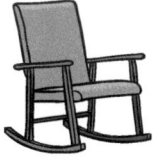

rocking chair

rocking chair

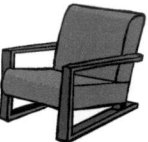

armchair

armchair

book
book

blanket
blanket

decoration
decoration

firewood
firewood

film
film

hi-fi equipment
hi-fi equipment

key
key

newspaper
newspaper

painting
painting

poster
poster

radio
radio

notepad
notepad

hoover
hoover

cactus
cactus

candle
candle

kitchen

kitchen

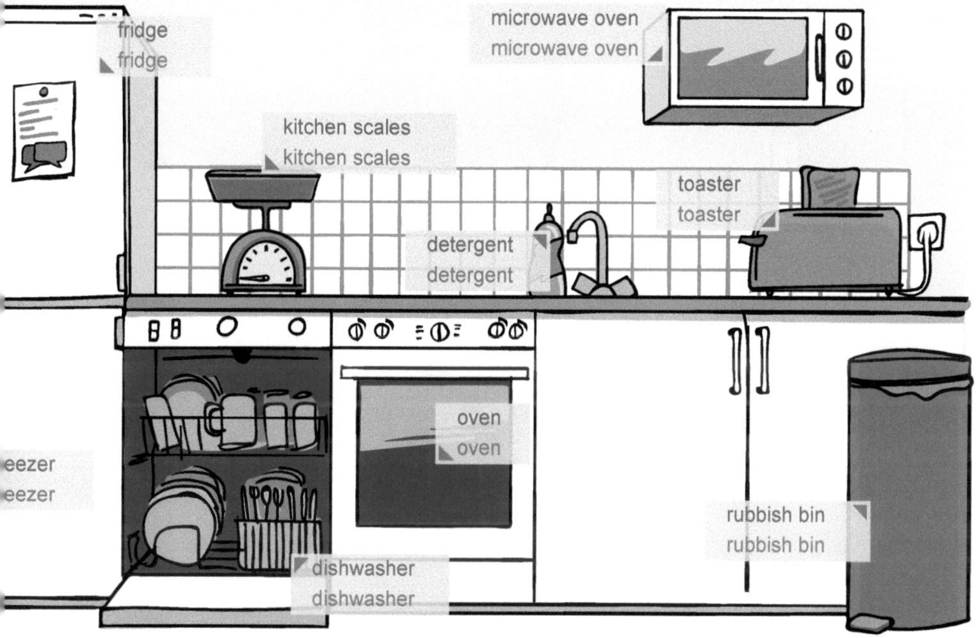
fridge
fridge
microwave oven
microwave oven
kitchen scales
kitchen scales
toaster
toaster
detergent
detergent
oven
oven
eezer
eezer
rubbish bin
rubbish bin
dishwasher
dishwasher

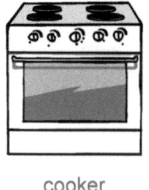

cooker

cooker

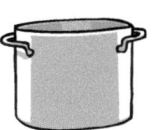

pot

pot

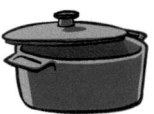

cast-iron pot

cast-iron pot

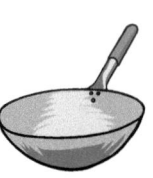

wok / kadai

wok / kadai

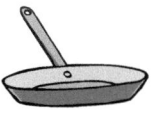

pan

pan

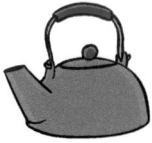

kettle

kettle

steamer

steamer

baking tray

baking tray

crockery

crockery

mug

mug

bowl

bowl

chopsticks

chopsticks

ladle

ladle

spatula

spatula

whisk

whisk

strainer

strainer

sieve

sieve

grater

grater

mortar

mortar

barbecue

barbecue

open fire

open fire

kitchen - kitchen

chopping board

chopping board

rolling pin

rolling pin

corkscrew

corkscrew

can

can

can opener

can opener

pot holder

pot holder

sink

sink

brush

brush

sponge

sponge

blender

blender

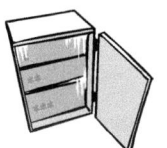

deep freezer

deep freezer

baby bottle

baby bottle

tap

tap

kitchen - kitchen

bathroom

bathroom

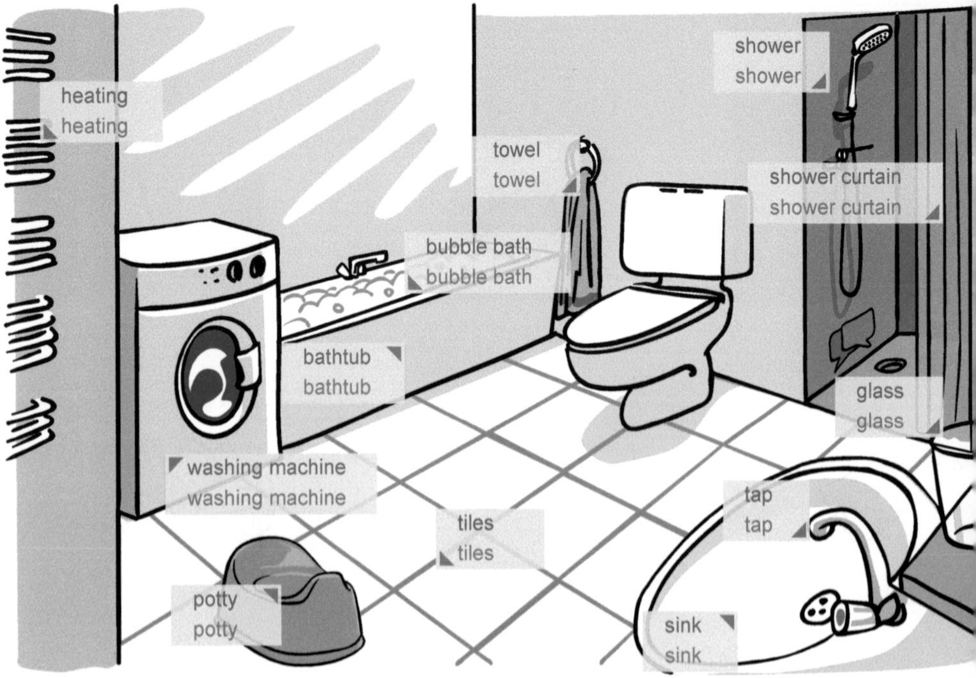
heating
heating
towel
towel
shower
shower
shower curtain
shower curtain
bubble bath
bubble bath
bathtub
bathtub
glass
glass
washing machine
washing machine
tiles
tiles
tap
tap
potty
potty
sink
sink

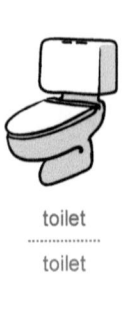

toilet

toilet

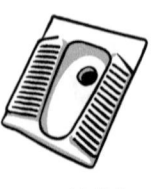

squat toilet

squat toilet

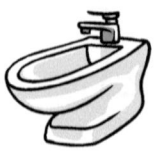

bidet

bidet

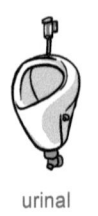

urinal

urinal

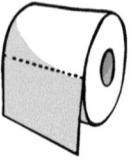

toilet paper

toilet paper

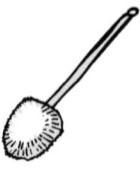

toilet brush

toilet brush

toothbrush

toothbrush

toothpaste

toothpaste

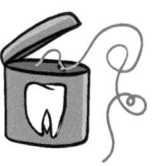

dental floss

dental floss

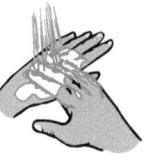

wash

wash

handheld shower

handheld shower

douche

douche

basin

basin

back brush

back brush

soap

soap

shower gel

shower gel

shampoo

shampoo

flannel

flannel

drain

drain

cream

cream

deodorant

deodorant

mirror

mirror

hand mirror

hand mirror

razor

razor

shaving foam

shaving foam

aftershave

aftershave

comb

comb

brush

brush

hair dryer

hair dryer

hairspray

hairspray

makeup

makeup

lipstick

lipstick

nail varnish

nail varnish

cotton wool

cotton wool

nail scissors

nail scissors

perfume

perfume

bathroom - bathroom

washbag

washbag

stool

stool

weighing scale

weighing scale

bathrobe

bathrobe

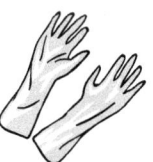

rubber gloves

rubber gloves

tampon

tampon

sanitary towel

sanitary towel

chemical toilet

chemical toilet

child's room
child's room

alarm clock
alarm clock
cuddly toy
cuddly toy
toy car
toy car
rattle
rattle
doll's house
doll's house
present
present

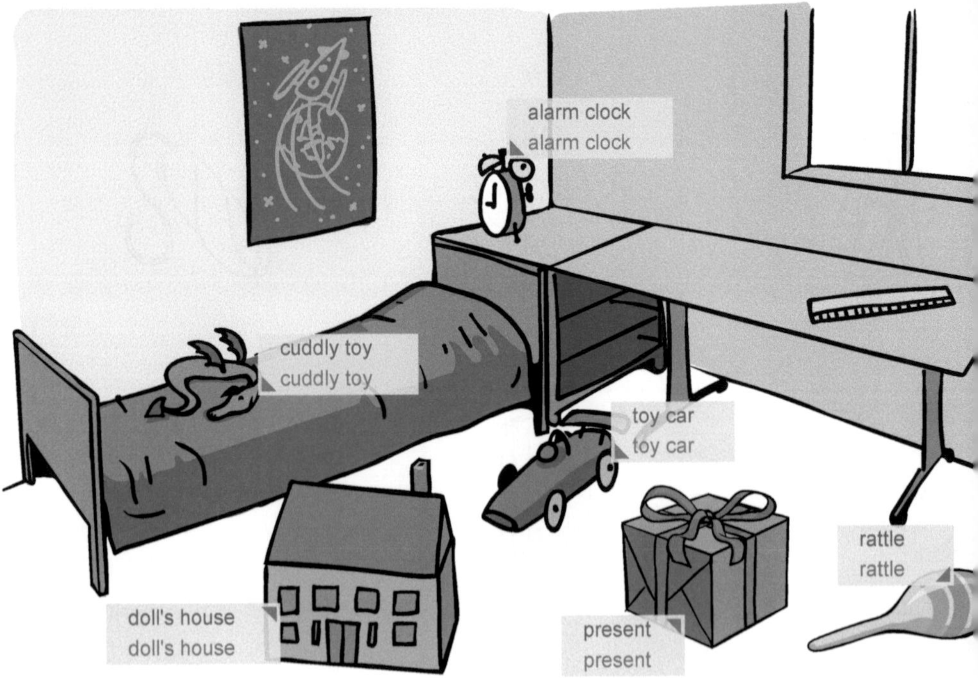

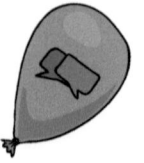

balloon
balloon

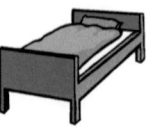

bed
bed

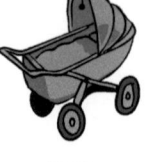

pram
pram

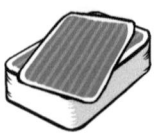

deck of cards
deck of cards

jigsaw
jigsaw

SUPER MEGA

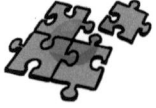

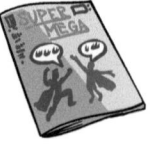

comic
comic

lego bricks
lego bricks

building blocks
building blocks

action figure
action figure

romper suit
babygrow

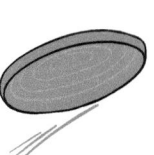

Frisbee
frisbee

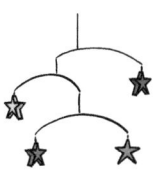

mobile
mobile

board game
board game

dice
dice

model train set
model train set

dummy
dummy

party
party

picture book
picture book

ball
ball

doll
doll

play
play

sandpit

sandpit

swing

swing

toys

toys

video game console

video game console

tricycle

tricycle

teddy bear

teddy bear

wardrobe

wardrobe

clothing

clothing

socks

socks

stockings

stockings

tights

tights

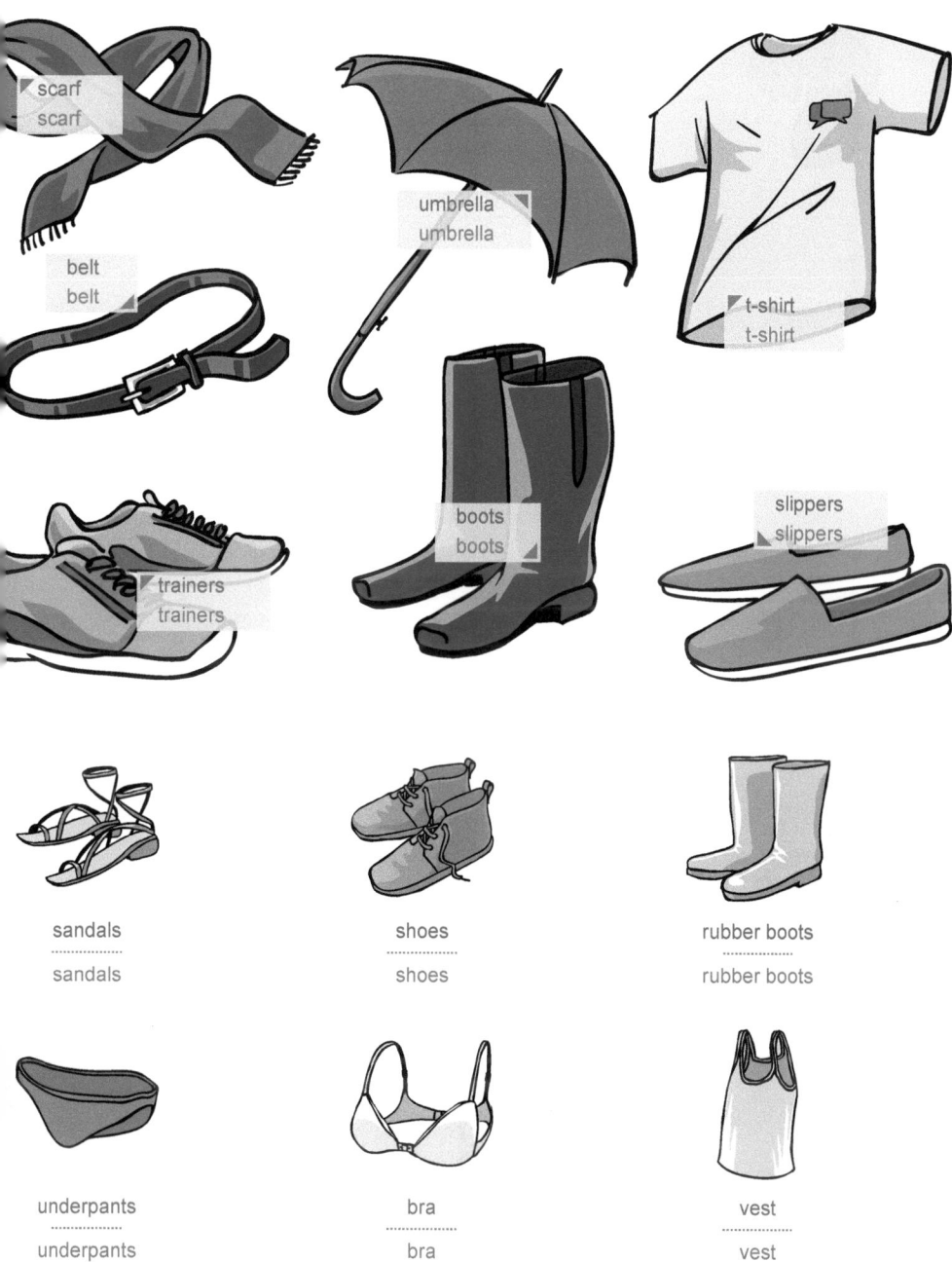

scarf
scarf

umbrella
umbrella

t-shirt
t-shirt

belt
belt

boots
boots

slippers
slippers

trainers
trainers

sandals
sandals

shoes
shoes

rubber boots
rubber boots

underpants
underpants

bra
bra

vest
vest

clothing - clothing

body
body

trousers
trousers

jeans
jeans

skirt
skirt

blouse
blouse

shirt
shirt

pullover
pullover

hoodie
hoodie

blazer
blazer

jacket
jacket

coat
coat

raincoat
raincoat

costume
costume

dress
dress

wedding dress
wedding dress

suit

suit

nightgown

nightgown

pyjamas

pyjamas

sari

sari

headscarf

headscarf

turban

turban

burqa

burqa

kaftan

kaftan

abaya

abaya

swimsuit

swimsuit

trunks

trunks

shorts

shorts

tracksuit

tracksuit

apron

apron

gloves

gloves

button
button

glasses
glasses

bracelet
bracelet

necklace
necklace

ring
ring

earring
earring

cap
cap

coat hanger
coat hanger

hat
hat

tie
tie

zipper
zip

helmet
helmet

braces
braces

school uniform
school uniform

uniform
uniform

bib

bib

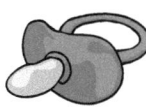

dummy

dummy

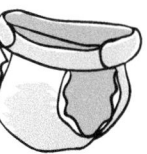

nappy

nappy

office

office

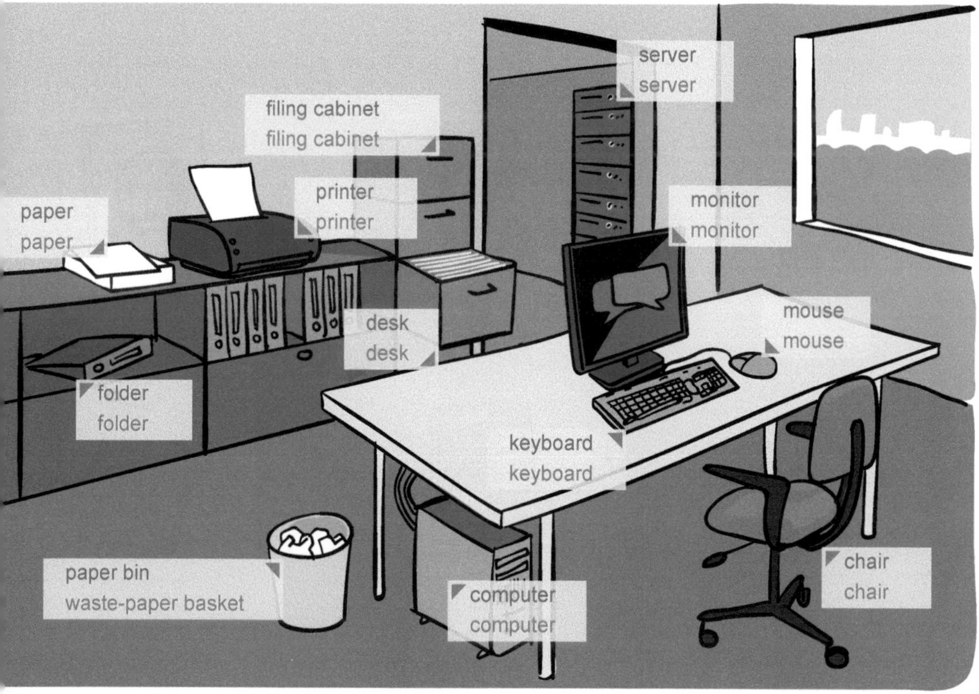

server
server

filing cabinet
filing cabinet

printer
printer

paper
paper

monitor
monitor

mouse
mouse

desk
desk

folder
folder

keyboard
keyboard

chair
chair

paper bin
waste-paper basket

computer
computer

coffee mug

coffee mug

calculator

calculator

internet

internet

laptop	letter	message
laptop	letter	message

mobile	network	photocopier
mobile	network	photocopier

software	telephone	plug socket
software	telephone	plug socket
	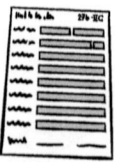	
fax machine	form	document
fax machine	form	document

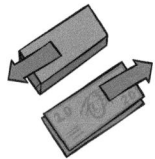

buy

buy

pay

pay

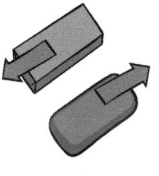

trade

trade

money

money

dollar

dollar

euro

euro

yen

yen

rouble

rouble

Swiss franc

Swiss franc

renminbi yuan

renminbi yuan

rupee

rupee

cashpoint

cashpoint

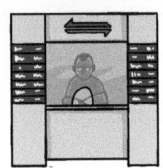

bureau de change

bureau de change

gold

gold

silver

silver

oil

oil

energy

energy

price

price

contract

contract

tax

tax

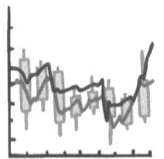

stock

stock

work

work

employee

employee

employer

employer

factory

factory

shop

shop

police officer
police officer

fireman
fireman

cook
cook

doctor
doctor

pilot
pilot

gardener
gardener

carpenter
carpenter

seamstress
seamstress

judge
judge

chemist
chemist

actor
actor

bus driver

bus driver

taxi driver

taxi driver

fisherman

fisherman

cleaning lady

cleaning lady

roofer

roofer

waiter

waiter

hunter

hunter

painter

painter

baker

baker

electrician

electrician

builder

builder

engineer

engineer

butcher

butcher

plumber

plumber

postman

postman

soldier

soldier

architect

architect

cashier

cashier

florist

florist

hairdresser

hairdresser

conductor

conductor

mechanic

mechanic

captain

captain

dentist

dentist

scientist

scientist

rabbi

rabbi

imam

imam

monk

monk

clergyman

clergyman

tools
tools

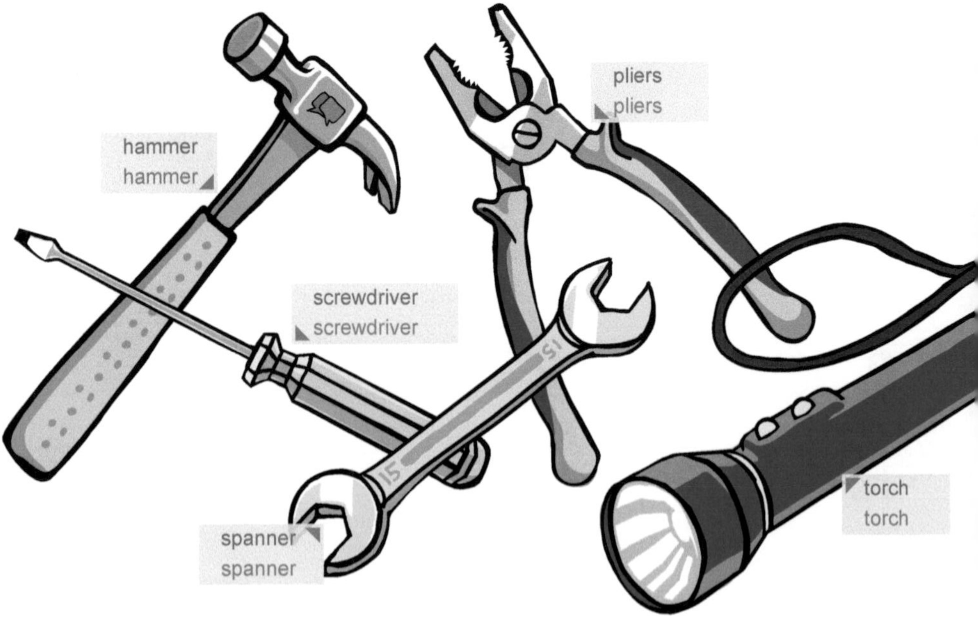

pliers
pliers
hammer
hammer
screwdriver
screwdriver
torch
torch
spanner
spanner

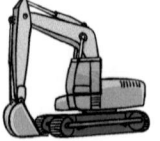

digger

digger

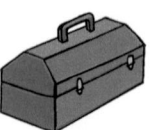

toolbox

toolbox

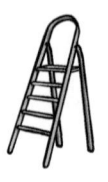

ladder

ladder

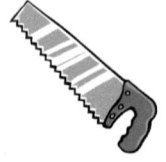

saw

saw

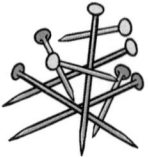

nails

nails

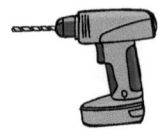

drill

drill

repair

repair

shovel

shovel

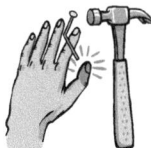

Damn!

Damn!

dustpan

dustpan

paint pot

paint pot

screws

screws

musical instruments
musical instruments

loudspeaker
loudspeaker

drum kit
drum kit

guitar
guitar

double bass
double bass

trumpet
trumpet

piano

piano

violin

violin

bass

bass

timpani

timpani

drums

drums

keyboard

keyboard

saxophone

saxophone

flute

flute

microphone

microphone

tiger
tiger

entrance
entrance

cage
cage

zebra
zebra

animal feed
animal feed

panda
panda

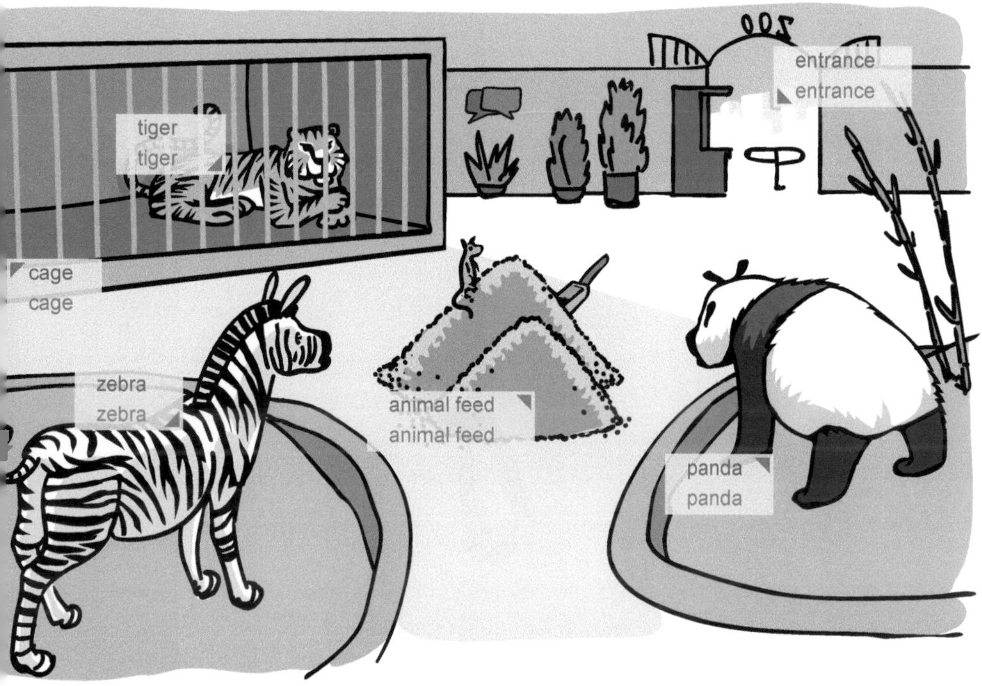

animals
animals

elephant
elephant

kangaroo
kangaroo

rhino
rhino

gorilla
gorilla

bear
bear

camel

camel

ostrich

ostrich

lion

lion

monkey

monkey

flamingo

flamingo

parrot

parrot

polar bear

polar bear

penguin

penguin

shark

shark

peacock

peacock

snake

snake

crocodile

crocodile

zookeeper

zookeeper

seal

seal

jaguar

jaguar

pony
pony

leopard
leopard

hippo
hippo

giraffe
giraffe

eagle
eagle

boar
boar

fish
fish

turtle
turtle

walrus
walrus

fox
fox

gazelle
gazelle

American football
American football

cycling
cycling

tennis
tennis

basketball
basketball

swimming
swimming

boxing
boxing

ice hockey
ice hockey

football
football

badminton
badminton

athletics
athletics

handball
handball

skiing
skiing

polo
polo

activities
activities

laugh
laugh
jump
jump
hug
hug
walk
walk
sing
sing
dream
dream
pray
pray
kiss
kiss

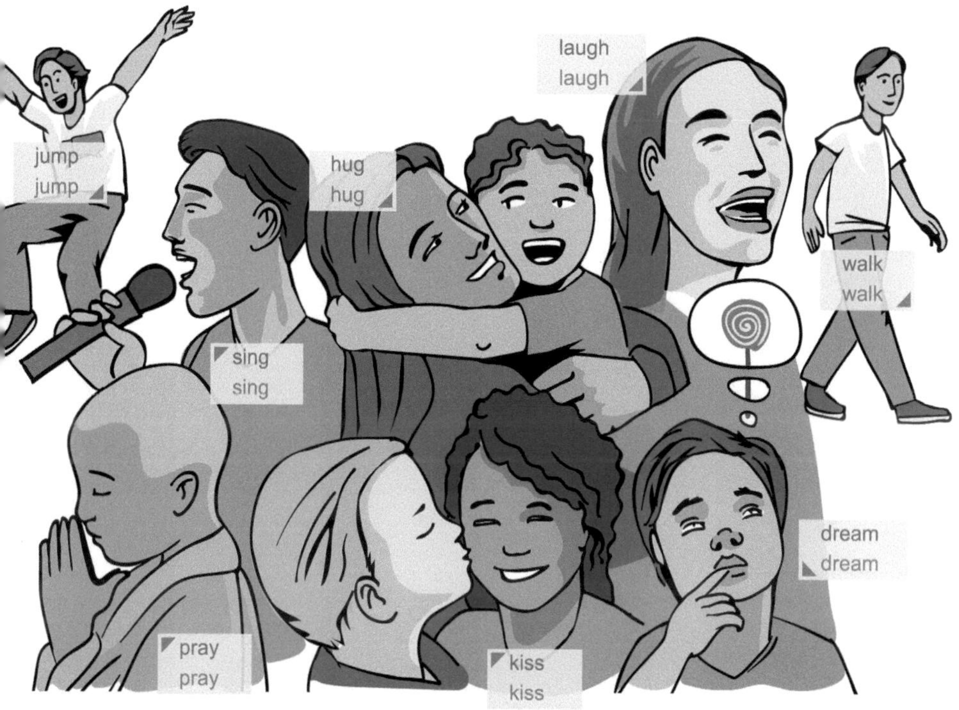

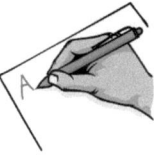

write
write

draw
draw

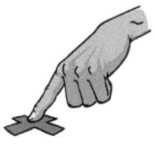

show
show

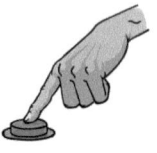

push
push

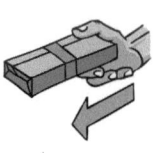

give
give

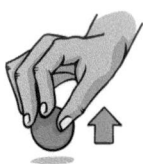

take
take

have

have

do

do

be

be

stand

stand

run

run

pull

pull

throw

throw

fall

fall

lie

lie

wait

wait

carry

carry

sit

sit

get dressed

get dressed

sleep

sleep

wake up

wake up

activities - activities

look at

look at

cry

cry

stroke

stroke

comb

comb

talk

talk

understand

understand

ask

ask

listen

listen

drink

drink

eat

eat

tidy up

tidy up

love

love

cook

cook

drive

drive

fly

fly

activities - activities

sail

sail

calculate

calculate

read

read

learn

learn

work

work

marry

marry

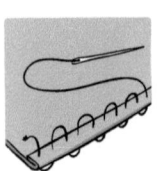

sew

sew

brush teeth

brush teeth

kill

kill

smoke

smoke

send

send

family

family

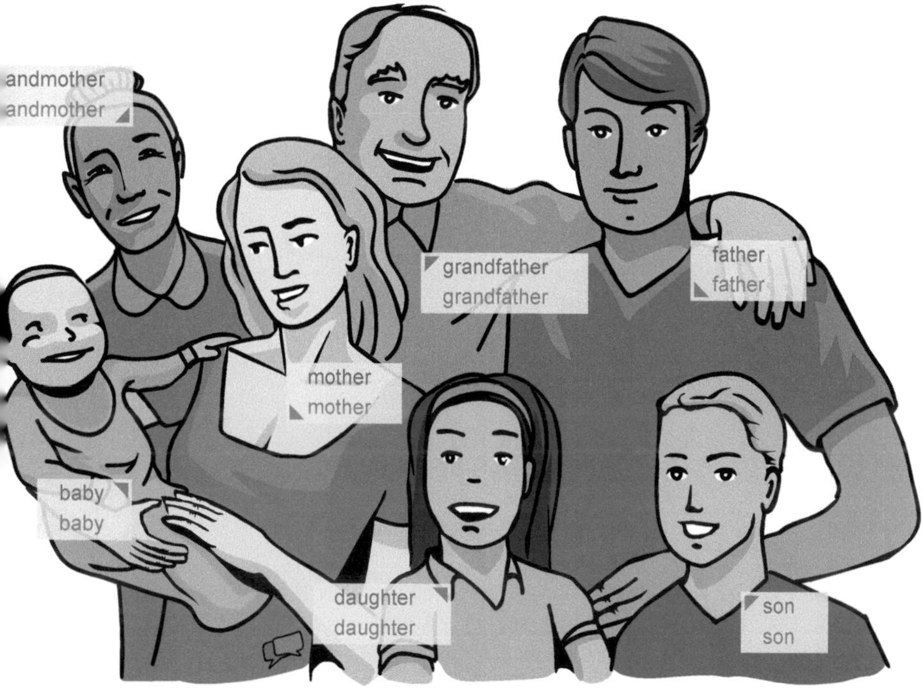
andmother
andmother
grandfather
grandfather
father
father
mother
mother
baby
baby
daughter
daughter
son
son

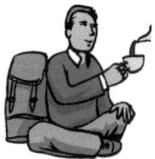

guest

guest

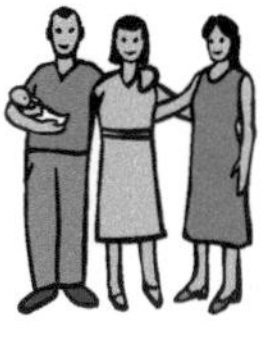

aunt

aunt

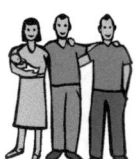

uncle

uncle

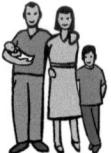

brother

brother

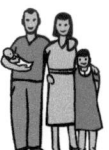

sister

sister

body

body

forehead
forehead
eye
eye
shoulder
shoulder
finger
finger
face
face
chin
chin
hand
hand
leg
leg
breast
breast
arm
arm

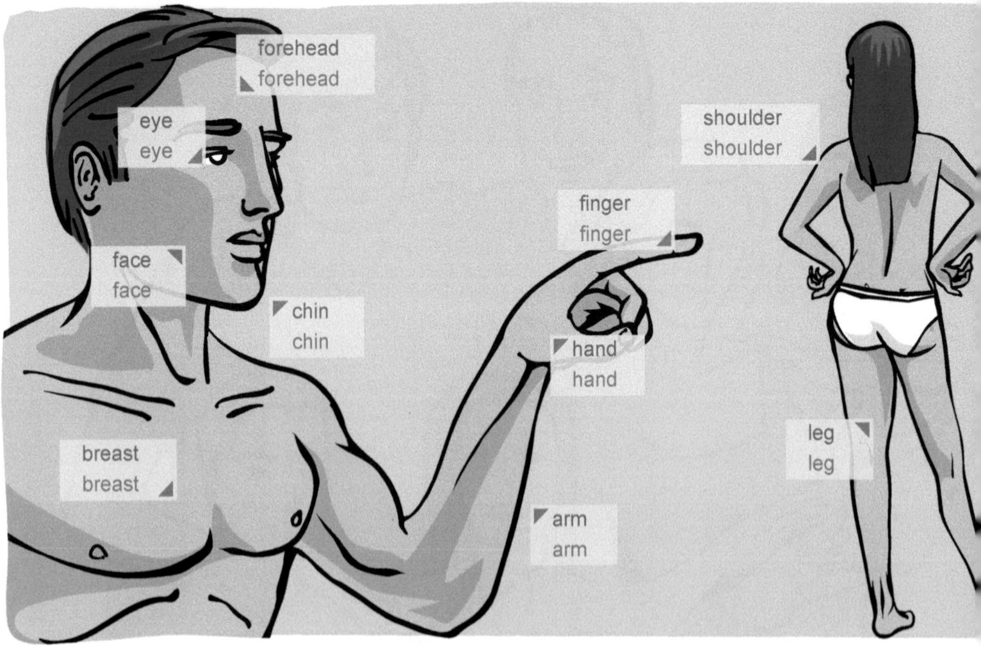

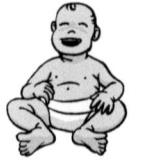

baby

baby

man

man

woman

woman

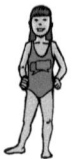

girl

girl

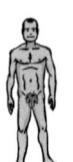

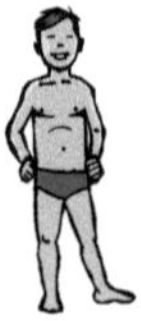

boy

boy

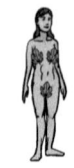

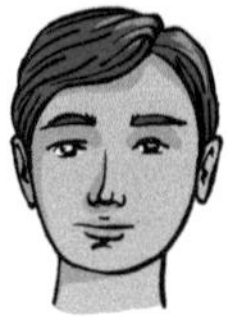

head

head

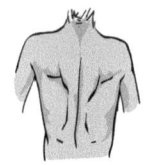

back
....
back

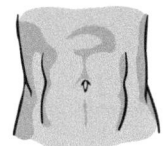

belly
....
belly

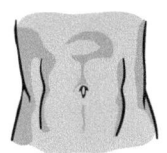

belly button
....
belly button

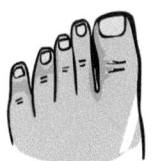

toe
....
toe

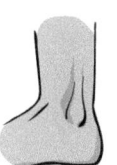

heel
....
heel

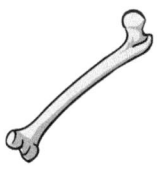

bone
....
bone

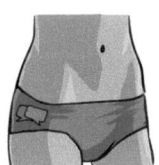

hip
....
hip

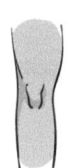

knee
....
knee

elbow
....
elbow

nose
....
nose

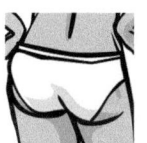

bottom
....
bottom

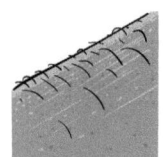

skin
....
skin

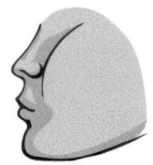

cheek
....
cheek

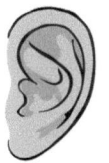

ear
....
ear

lip
....
lip

body - body

mouth

mouth

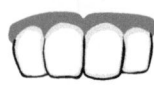

tooth

tooth

tongue

tongue

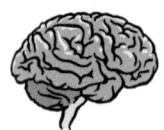

brain

brain

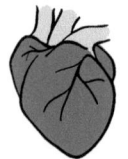

heart

heart

muscle

muscle

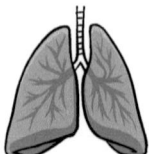

lung

lung

liver

liver

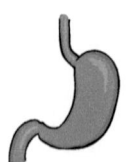

stomach

stomach

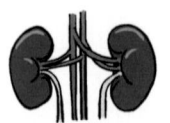

kidneys

kidneys

sex

sex

condom

condom

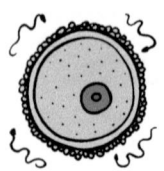

ovum

ovum

semen

semen

pregnancy

pregnancy

body - body

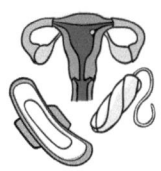

menstruation

menstruation

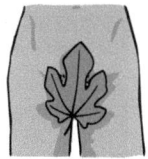

vagina

vagina

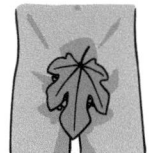

penis

penis

eyebrow

eyebrow

hair

hair

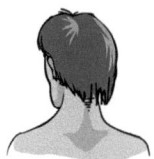

neck

neck

hospital

hospital

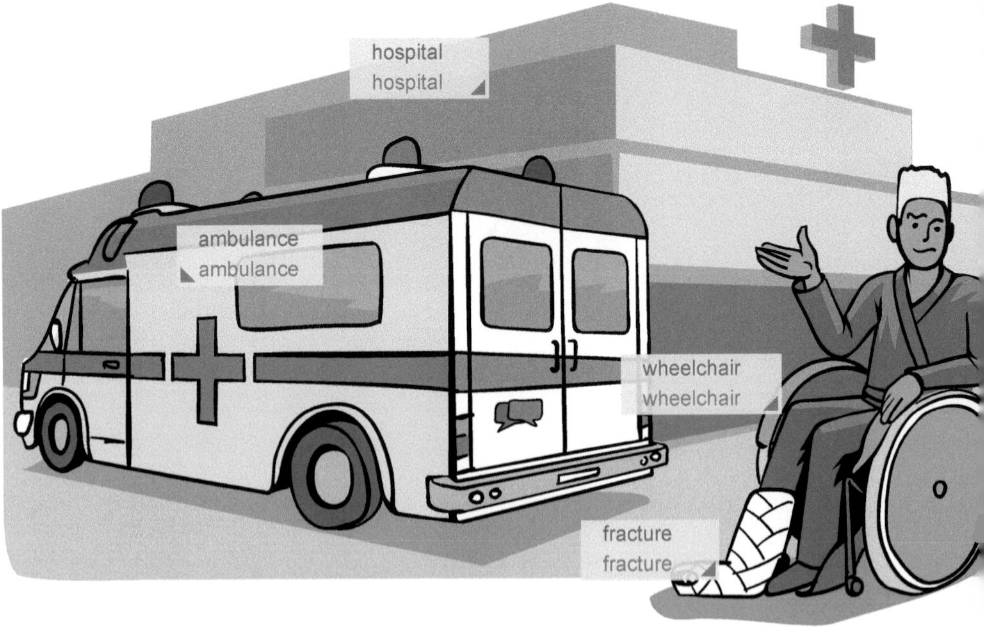

hospital
hospital
ambulance
ambulance
wheelchair
wheelchair
fracture
fracture

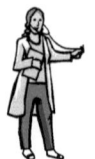

doctor

doctor

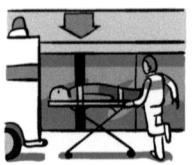

emergency room

emergency room

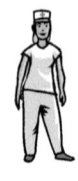

nurse

nurse

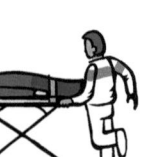

emergency

emergency

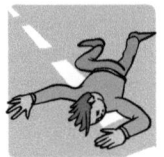

unconscious

unconscious

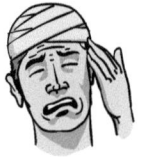

pain

pain

injury

injury

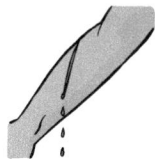

bleeding

bleeding

heart attack

heart attack

stroke

stroke

allergy

allergy

cough

cough

fever

fever

flu

flu

diarrhoea

diarrhoea

headache

headache

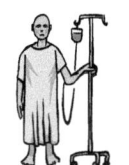

cancer

cancer

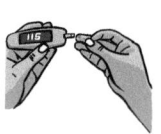

diabetes

diabetes

surgeon

surgeon

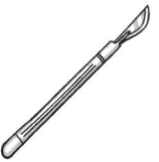

scalpel

scalpel

operation

operation

hospital - hospital

CT
CT

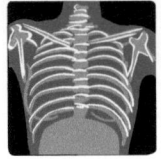

x-ray
x-ray

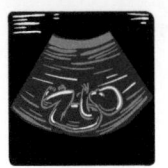

ultrasound
ultrasound

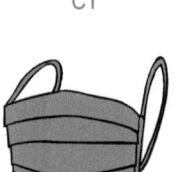

face mask
face mask

disease
disease

waiting room
waiting room

crutch
crutch

plaster
plaster

bandage
bandage

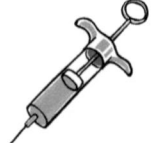

injection
injection

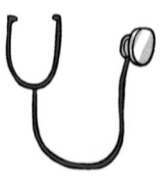

stethoscope
stethoscope

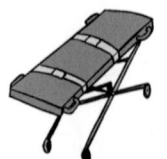

stretcher
stretcher

clinical thermometer
clinical thermometer

birth
birth

overweight
overweight

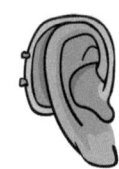

hearing aid

hearing aid

disinfectant

disinfectant

infection

infection

virus

virus

HIV / AIDS

HIV / AIDS

medicine

medicine

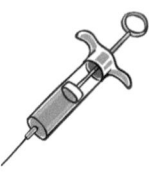

vaccination

vaccination

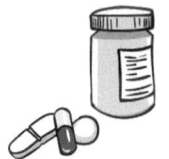

tablets

tablets

pill

pill

emergency call

emergency call

blood pressure monitor

blood pressure monitor

sick / healthy

ill / healthy

Help!

Help!

alarm

alarm

assault

assault

attack

attack

danger

danger

emergency exit

emergency exit

Fire!

Fire!

fire extinguisher

fire extinguisher

accident

accident

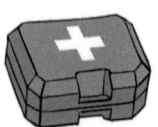

first-aid kit

first-aid kit

SOS

SOS

police

police

Europe

Europe

North America

North America

South America

South America

Africa

Africa

Asia

Asia

Australia

Australia

Atlantic

Atlantic

Pacific

Pacific

Indian Ocean

Indian Ocean

Antarctic Ocean

Antarctic Ocean

Arctic Ocean

Arctic Ocean

North Pole

North Pole

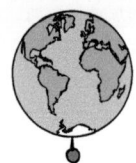

South Pole
....
South Pole

Antarctica
....
Antarctica

Earth
....
Earth

land
....
land

sea
....
sea

island
....
island

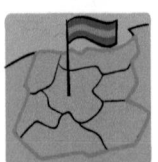

nation
....
nation

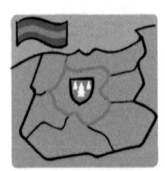

state
....
state

clock face

clock face

hour hand

hour hand

minute hand

minute hand

second hand

second hand

What time is it?

What time is it?

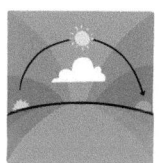

day

day

time

time

now

now

digital watch

digital watch

minute

minute

hour

hour

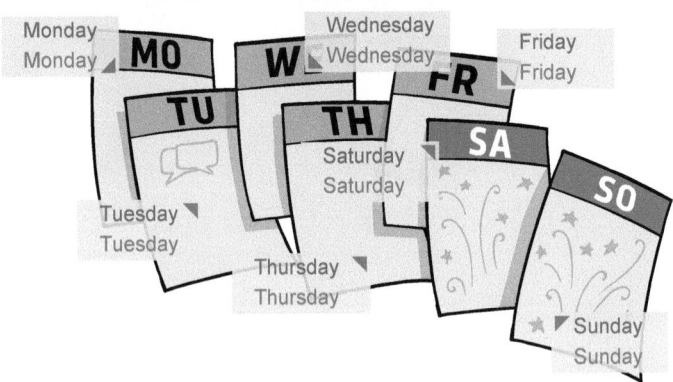

yesterday

yesterday

today

today

tomorrow

tomorrow

morning

morning

noon

noon

evening

evening

business days

business days

weekend

weekend

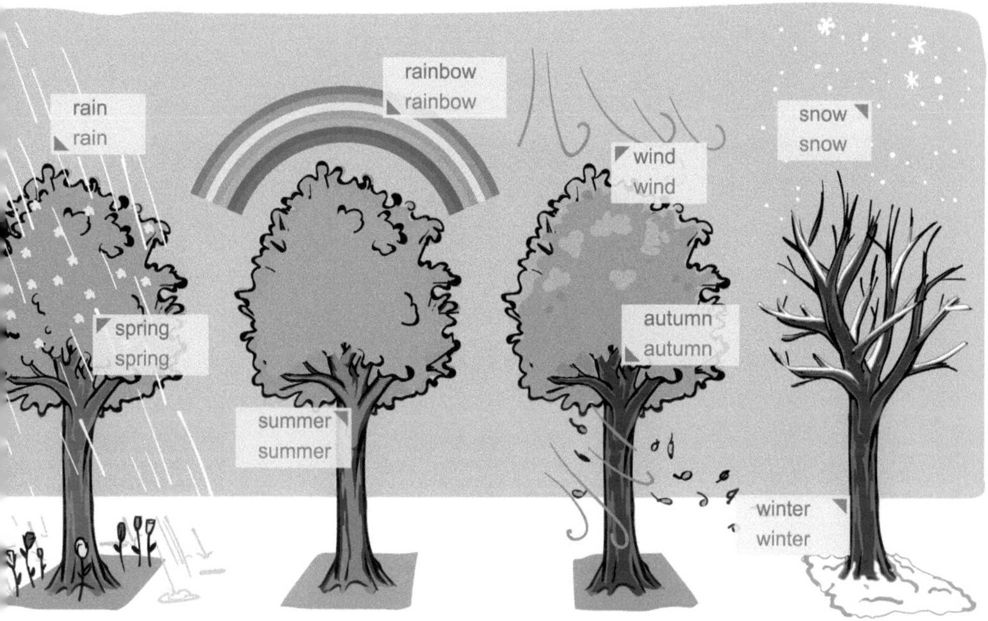

rain
rain
rainbow
rainbow
wind
wind
snow
snow
spring
spring
summer
summer
autumn
autumn
winter
winter

4.APRIL 11°
5.APRIL 4°
6.APRIL 13°
7.APRIL 8°
8.APRIL 10°

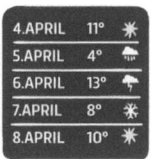

weather forecast

weather forecast

F
C
120
90
60
30
0
-30
40
30
20
10
0
-10
-20

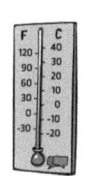

thermometer

thermometer

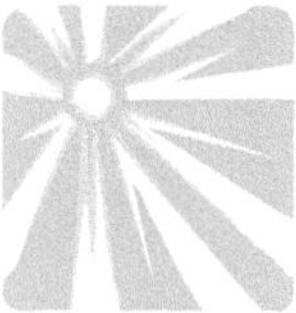

sunshine

sunshine

cloud

cloud

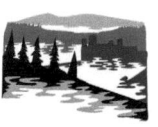

fog

fog

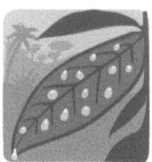

humidity

humidity

lightning

lightning

thunder

thunder

storm

storm

hail

hail

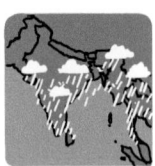

monsoon

monsoon

flood

flood

ice

ice

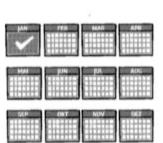

January

January

February

February

March

March

April

April

May

May

June

June

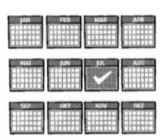

July

July

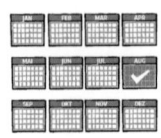

August

August

year - year

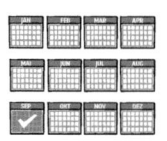

September
....
September

October
....
October

November
....
November

December
....
December

shapes
shapes

circle
....
circle

square
....
square

rectangle
....
rectangle

triangle
....
triangle

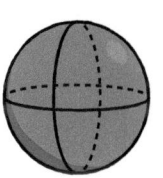

sphere
....
sphere

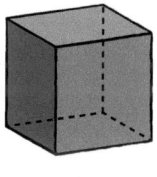

cube
....
cube

white
....
white

yellow
....
yellow

orange
....
orange

pink
....
pink

red
....
red

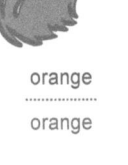

purple
....
purple

blue
....
blue

green
....
green

brown
....
brown

grey
....
grey

black
....
black

a lot / a little

a lot / a little

angry / calm

angry / calm

beautiful / ugly

beautiful / ugly

beginning / end

beginning / end

big / small

big / small

bright / dark

bright / dark

brother / sister

brother / sister

clean / dirty

clean / dirty

complete / incomplete

complete / incomplete

day / night

day / night

dead / alive

dead / alive

wide / narrow

wide / narrow

edible / inedible
....
edible / inedible

evil / nice
....
evil / kind

excited / bored
....
excited / bored

fat / thin
....
fat / thin

first / last
....
first / last

friend / enemy
....
friend / enemy

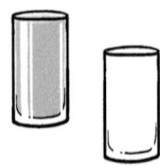

full / empty
....
full / empty

hard / soft
....
hard / soft

heavy / light
....
heavy / light

hunger / thirst
....
hunger / thirst

sick / healthy
....
ill / healthy

illegal / legal
....
illegal / legal

intelligent / stupid
....
intelligent / stupid

left / right
....
left / right

near / far
....
near / far

opposites - opposites

new / used

new / used

nothing / something

nothing / something

old / young

old / young

on / off

on / off

open / closed

open / closed

quiet / loud

quiet / loud

rich / poor

rich / poor

right / wrong

right / wrong

rough / smooth

rough / smooth

sad / happy

sad / happy

short / long

short / long

slow / fast

slow / fast

wet / dry

wet / dry

warm / cool

warm / cool

war / peace

war / peace

0

zero

zero

1

one

one

2

two

two

3

three

three

4

four

four

5

five

five

6

six

six

7

seven

seven

8

eight

eight

9

nine

nine

10

ten

ten

11

eleven

eleven

12

twelve

twelve

13

thirteen

thirteen

14

fourteen

fourteen

15

fifteen

fifteen

16

sixteen

sixteen

17

seventeen

seventeen

18

eighteen

eighteen

19

nineteen

nineteen

20

twenty

twenty

100

hundred

hundred

1.000

thousand

thousand

1.000.000

million

million

languages

English

English

American English

American English

Mandarin Chinese

Chinese Mandarin

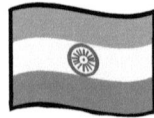

Hindi

Hindi

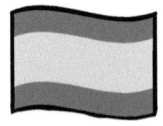

Spanish

Spanish

French

French

Arabic

Arabic

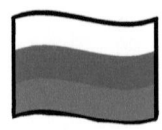

Russian

Russian

Portuguese

Portuguese

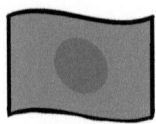

Bengali

Bengali

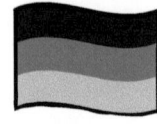

German

German

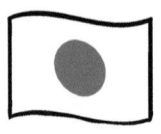

Japanese

Japanese

I

I

you

you

he / she / it

he / she / it

we

we

you

you

they

they

who?

who?

what?

what?

how?

how?

where?

where?

when?

when?

name

name

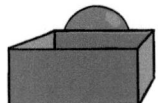

behind

behind

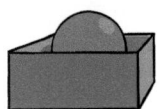

in

in

in front of

in front of

over

over

on

on

under

under

beside

beside

between

between

place

place